I'm Going To R...

These levels are meant only ~~as guides,~~
you and your child can best choose a book that's right.

Level 1: Kindergarten–Grade 1 . . . Ages 4–6
- word bank to highlight new words
- consistent placement of text to promote readability
- easy words and phrases
- simple sentences build to make simple stories
- art and design help new readers decode text

Level 2: Grade 1 . . . Ages 6–7
- word bank to highlight new words
- rhyming texts introduced
- more difficult words, but vocabulary is still limited
- longer sentences and longer stories
- designed for easy readability

Level 3: Grade 2 . . . Ages 7–8
- richer vocabulary of up to 200 different words
- varied sentence structure
- high-interest stories with longer plots
- designed to promote independent reading

Level 4: Grades 3 and up . . . Ages 8 and up
- richer vocabulary of more than 300 different words
- short chapters, multiple stories, or poems
- more complex plots for the newly independent reader
- emphasis on reading for meaning

LEVEL 3

Library of Congress Cataloging-in-Publication Data Available

2 4 6 8 10 9 7 5 3 1

Published by Sterling Publishing Co., Inc.
387 Park Avenue South, New York, NY 10016
Text copyright © 2005 by Harriet Ziefert Inc.
Illustrations copyright © 2005 by Santiago Cohen
Distributed in Canada by Sterling Publishing
c/o Canadian Manda Group, 165 Dufferin Street
Toronto, Ontario, Canada M6K 3H6
Distributed in Great Britain and Europe by Chris Lloyd at Orca Book
Services, Stanley House, Fleets Lane, Poole BH15 3AJ, England
Distributed in Australia by Capricorn Link (Australia) Pty. Ltd.
P.O. Box 704, Windsor, NSW 2756, Australia

I'm Going To Read is a trademark of Sterling Publishing Co., Inc.

Printed in China

Sterling ISBN 1-4027-2103-X

Go Away, Crows!

Pictures by
Santiago Cohen

Sterling Publishing Co., Inc.
New York

**Matt and Isabel lived
in a small house.**

It was a nice house—
and they liked it.

One day Isabel heard loud noises.
CAW! CAW! CAW! CAW!
She said, "Matt, look at those crows.
I do not like them."

"Why not?"
Matt asked.

"This is OUR house," said Isabel. "I don't
want to share it with crows."

But the big black crows
liked Isabel's house.

They liked the fence.
They liked the steps.
They liked the porch.

Every day the crows came.
Every day Isabel yelled,
"Go away, crows!
Go away to your own house!"

**But Isabel did not
let him finish his sentence.
She had an idea of her own.**

Isabel got a bucket
of water.

Watch me.
Watch me sca
those crows.

Then she dumped it!

The crows went away.
But they came back!

The crows went away.
But they came back!

I have an idea.
We can keep the crows
away if . . .

But Isabel did not let him
finish the sentence.

I have an idea
of my own.
I'm smart—smarter
than those crows.

Matt asked, "Are you
sure a sign will keep
the crows away?"

Isabel said, "I'm sure it will.
I have good ideas.
And this is one of my best."

Later Matt and Isabel went to bed.

In the morning Isabel heard—

CAW! CAW! CAW! CAW!

She yelled at the crows.

Matt thought he could help.
He told Isabel to wait.

Matt went to the basement.

He found an old sheet . . .

a broom . . .

a ball of string . . .

a marker . . .
and a pair of gloves.

Matt heard Isabel call:
"Where are you?
What's taking so long?"

Just wait a minute.
I'll be right there.

Isabel waited and waited . . .
until she got tired of waiting.
She shouted from the window.

There was no answer from Matt.
But Isabel saw something strange
moving through the garden.

Then Isabel and Matt had
the best idea of all.

"Let's have a part
A party for two.
No crows allowed